Henry Kreisel Lecture Series

1

From Mushkegowuk to New Orleans:
A Mixed Blood Highway

by Joseph Boyden

ISBN 978-1-897126-29-5

2

The Old Lost Land of Newfoundland:
Family, Memory, Fiction, and Myth

by Wayne Johnston

ISBN 978-1-897126-35-6

3

J'écris comme je vis / I Write as I Live

by Dany Laferrière

ISBN 978-1-897126-43-3

[AVAILABLE 2010]

Henry Kreisel Lecture Series

NeWest press I CLC

WAYNE JOHNSTON

THE OLD LOST LAND

of NEWFOUNDLAND:
Family, Memory, Fiction, and Myth

Library and Archives Canada Cataloguing in Publication
Johnston, Wayne, 1958-
The old lost land of Newfoundland : family, memory, fiction, and myth /
Wayne Johnston.
(Henry Kreisel lecture series 2)
Co-published by the Canadian Literature Centre=Centre de littérature
canadienne.
ISBN 978-1-897126-35-6
1. Newfoundland and Labrador--History--Anecdotes. 2. Newfoundland
and Labrador--Social life and customs. I. Canadian Literature Centre II.
Title. III. Series.
FC2161.8.J65 2009   971.8   C2008-907438-6

Editor for the Board: Diane Bessai
Cover design: Natalie Olsen
Interior design: Natalie Olsen
Author photo: Jerry Bauer

¶ The text face in this book is Cartier Book Pro, Rod McDonald's revival of the distinctively Canadian typeface Cartier, originally designed by Carl Dair in 1967. ¶ The sans serif used to mark additional comments made by Wayne Johnston during his lecture is Parisine, which was designed by the French typographer Jean-François Porchez in 1999.

The excerpt on pages 45 – 47 is from Wayne Johnston's *The Colony of Unrequited Dreams* and was reproduced by permission from its publisher.

 Canada Council for the Arts Conseil des Arts du Canada   Canadian Heritage Patrimoine canadien   Alberta Foundation for the Arts   edmonton arts council

The Canadian Literature Centre acknowledges the support of the Alberta Foundation for the Arts for the Henry Kreisel Lecture delivered by Wayne Johnston in March 2008 at the University of Alberta.

NeWest Press acknowledges the support of the Canada Council for the Arts, the Alberta Foundation for the Arts, and the Edmonton Arts Council for our publishing program. We also acknowledge the financial support of the Government of Canada through the Book Publishing Industry Development Program (BPDIP).

CLC

Canadian Literature Centre
3-5 Humanities Centre
University of Alberta
Edmonton, Alberta, Canada T6G 2E5
780.492.9505
www.arts.ualberta.ca/clc

NEWEST PRESS

201, 8540 109 Street
Edmonton, Alberta T6G 1E6
780.432.9427
www.newestpress.com

1 2 3 4 5 12 11 10 09
printed and bound in Canada

FOREWORD

Henry Kreisel fled Nazi Austria at the age of sixteen and spent the next three years of his life in internment camps in England and eastern Canada. From such difficult national beginnings — as an "enemy alien" — he went on to become the University of Alberta's most distinguished working humanist. As a teacher of English and Comparative Literature, he was beloved for his capacity to change hearts and challenge minds. As Department Head and later Vice-President Academic, he was admired for his capacious open-mindedness — one of his many transformative accomplishments was to introduce the first course in Canadian Literature to the University of Alberta. As a creative writer, he was read not only for his storytelling but for his ability to unsettle the cognitive landscape. His novels and stories brought another kind of global consciousness into the field of Canadian writing.

The University of Alberta's Canadian Literature Centre / Centre de littérature canadienne came into existence in 2006 with a mandate to bring book people together — teachers, students, scholars, collectors, librarians, authors, publishers, readers of every kind — and to foster a critical attitude that understands literature as a necessary participant in contemporary public debate. That mandate sits at the heart of the annual Henry Kreisel Lecture, which is now being published in collaboration with NeWest Press — a literary publishing house that Henry Kreisel himself helped found over thirty years ago.

The Henry Kreisel Lectures celebrate the enduring presence of a scholar, teacher, and social critic who reached beyond the ivory tower and its disciplinary boundaries toward a wider community of minds. They celebrate the public lecture itself as a forum for open, inclusive, critical thinking. They celebrate the transformative capacity of literary language to foster in readers a commitment to social justice. Finally, they celebrate the inalienable contribution of imaginative writing to the project of social change.

Stephen Slemon

Former Director, Canadian Literature Centre

Professor, English and Film Studies

University of Alberta

January 2009

INTRODUCTION

I'm very pleased to have been asked to introduce Wayne Johnston tonight, but before I begin that very pleasant task I have to gratefully acknowledge some of the many people who have made it possible for us to host him here at the University of Alberta. First, always, thanks are due to my colleague Stephen Slemon, under whose really brilliant directorship of the Canadian Literature Centre the annual Kreisel lectures have been re-established. Stephen's enthusiasm and energy infuses everything we do at the Centre, and this event could not have happened without him. I would also like to convey sincere thanks to Sarah Jeffries, Liz Greenaway, and Michele Jackson, to whom we are indebted for all the preparations for this evening's lecture; their work is evident in every aspect of this event and we are all enormously grateful to them. Thanks again to the Executive Committee of the Canadian Literature Centre, the Centre's generous donors, the Alberta Foundation for the Arts for supporting this lecture series, and to the Faculty of Arts for their commitment to the Centre's work. Thanks to Laurie Greenwood, always a supporter of the Centre's work and herself a kind of dynamic centre for the promotion and development of Canadian literature here in Edmonton. Thanks also to Mr. Leo Furey, who kindly provided advice and assistance to me when the Centre began the arrangements for this evening. And, finally, thanks to my aunt and uncle, Mary and Ged Blackmore, for their always wise and gracious guidance, and most of all for giving me Wayne Johnston's phone number.

Wayne Johnston is one of the best-known and most respected writers in Canada. Born and raised in Goulds, Newfoundland, he received a BA from the Memorial University of Newfoundland and an MA in Creative Writing from the University of New Brunswick. Beginning his career as a reporter for the *St. John's Daily News*, he published his first novel, *The Story of Bobby O'Malley*, in 1985, winning the W.H. Smith/Books in Canada First Novel Award that same year. Since then he has written another six novels and a memoir, *Baltimore's Mansion*, a book that, in 2000, won the Charles Taylor Prize, the most prestigious award in Canada for creative non-fiction. His 1990 novel, *The Divine Ryans*, which received the Thomas Raddall Atlantic Fiction Award, was made into a film, for which Johnston also wrote the screenplay. With the publication of *The Colony of Unrequited Dreams* in 1999, Wayne Johnston really erupted onto the literary scene. An epic story of Newfoundland's complicated colonial history, Johnston's fictional account of Joseph Smallwood's monumental and contentious gesture in bringing Newfoundland, as Smallwood infamously put it, "kicking and screaming into the twentieth century" met with immediate critical acclaim. Winner of the Raddall Award and the Canadian Authors Association Award for Fiction in 1999, *Colony* was shortlisted for the Giller Prize and the Governor-General's Award. It has since been named one of the one hundred most important books in Canadian history by *The Globe and Mail*. Johnston's most recent novel, *The Custodian of Paradise*, published in 2006, returns to the figure of Sheilagh Fielding, who emerged in *Colony* as one of the most compelling characters in Canadian fiction. Wayne Johnston is a contributing editor of *The Walrus* magazine and, since 2004, Distinguished Chair in Creative Writing at Hollins University in Virginia. In 2007, he received an honorary doctorate from Memorial University.

Wayne Johnston's talk tonight is entitled "The Old Lost Land of Newfoundland: Family, Memory, Fiction, and Myth." Readers of *The Colony of Unrequited Dreams* — or, indeed, any of Johnston's fiction — will recognize the image and the idea of a Newfoundland that is character-ized simultaneously in terms of what has been lost and of what remains always there, internalized or incorporated at the level of memory. This is the Newfoundland that Joey Smallwood sees upon his return from New York, the place "that you have never seen before but that seem[s] remind-ful of some not-quite-remembered other life" (211), and it is both culturally specific, with its own peculiar history, and metaphorical: Smallwood's memory and comprehension of what he describes as "the place as it had been [...] and as it would be" is something that might be understood as a part of the condition of being human. That is, that place of simultaneous past and future, loss and imminence is, in effect, in us, everywhere, and we are always poised, as Johnston reminds us, on the brink of both.

If you Google Wayne Johnston you will find that there is more than one. According to Wikipedia, Wayne Johnston may refer to a novelist or to a former Australian football player known as "The Dominator." Indeed, there is a Wayne Johnston website operated by someone who identifies himself as *not* being several Wayne Johnstons, beginning his list by noting that he's not the famous Canadian author. We are privileged tonight to have at the University of Alberta for this year's Kreisel lecture the one who *is* the famous Canadian author. Surely a dominator in this field of Canadian literature, a writer of extraordinary skill and grace, and the honoured guest of the Canadian Literature Centre, please join me in welcoming *our* Wayne Johnston.

Cecily Devereux

Member, CLC Executive Committee

Associate Professor, English and Film Studies

University of Alberta

February 2008

Works Cited

Johnston, Wayne. *The Colony of Unrequited Dreams.* Toronto: Knopf, 1999.

THE OLD LOST LAND OF NEWFOUNDLAND:
FAMILY, MEMORY, FICTION, AND MYTH

NEWFOUNDLAND became a province of Canada on March 31, 1949.

That is a historical fact.

Well, not quite. It's a historical misconception out of which my father and aunts and uncles have got a lot of mileage over the years.

The induction ceremonies — my father called them the "annexation hijinks" — were originally set for April 1, 1949. It occurred to no one at the federal level that April Fool's Day might not be the most appropriate of dates on which to celebrate (mourn, my father said) Newfoundland's joining with Confederation.

It was Joey Smallwood, the newly appointed premier,

who was already being called the father of Confederation, who brought it to the attention of the prime minister in Ottawa.

The date was then, at the eleventh hour, "changed," though in fact it was too late to really change it since all sorts of ceremonies had already been scheduled for April 1 on Parliament Hill and in St. John's.

But Prime Minister Louis St. Laurent amended the terms of union to read that Newfoundland would join the Dominion of Canada "immediately before the expiration of March 31, 1949."

My father said it was a pity that Newfoundland couldn't join Canada immediately *after* the expiration of Joey Smallwood, that being the only circumstance, my father said, under which he would be happy to see "the treacherous bastard live forever."

> He also poured scorn on the phrase "immediately before the expiration of," often holding forth at parties about what the anonymous phrase-maker could possibly have thought was the meaning of those words.
>
> "They have no meaning," my father would say. "Imagine a second. Now imagine dividing that second in half. And those halves in half, and so on and so on, for all eternity, and you will still have come no closer to anything that even approximates being 'immediately before the expiration of' any-thing, with the possible exception of your sanity. But whatever that purely hypothetical measure-ment of time is, the confederates knew they were

robbing us of that duration of independence. It
wasn't enough to 'win' the referendum. It wasn't
enough to declare April 1 Annexation Day. No,
they had to add an unimaginably small bit of insult
to injury, throw into the open wound the world's
tiniest grain of salt."

The ceremonies in Newfoundland and Ottawa took place
on April 1, and many people, especially those who, like
me, are descended from anti-confederates, still consider
April 1 to be induction day, a day on which some of my
relatives still wear black arm bands of mourning and
fly from their flag poles the Pink, White, and Green, the
so-called underground flag of Newfoundland.

I wear a tattoo of that flag on my upper right arm, not
as a protest but as a gesture of commemoration for all the
people who fought, and in one case may have died, for
everything they believed it to represent.

I was once asked to pose for the swimsuit edition
of *Saturday Night* magazine. I agreed. It was one
of those things that seems like a good idea at the
time, but which seems less and less like one as the
day of the actual event approaches.

I was photographed sitting in the backyard of
my house in Toronto wearing only an undershirt
and shorts, my Pink, White, and Green tattoo
prominently displayed and, beneath the tattoo, the
name "Clio," who was, and for my money still is,
The Muse of History.

The Pink, White, and Green, or "PWAG" as it is

sometimes referred to in my family with a kind of fond irony because it rhymes with "flag."

"Smallwood left us with nothing but a PWAG," my father and aunts and uncles often say. Many impossible-to-repeat-here variations on the acronym have been rung, with each letter standing for something it is not popularly known to stand for, such as "Premier With Awful Gas."

The Pink, White, and Green has been making something of a comeback in Newfoundland recently, especially in St. John's, the capital city where Confederation was opposed by a large majority. It flies from flagpoles, appears on T-shirts and other articles of clothing, and figures prominently in fresco-sized graffiti.

When I was a boy, a poem called "Fling Out the Flag" was often recited during parties, and at the end of them, "The Ode to Newfoundland", one verse of which reads: "As loved our fathers, so we love / Where once they stood we stand."

Our fathers. That line of the song always gave me cold shivers, even though I didn't quite understand why. When it came time to sing the Ode, all the grownups were teary-eyed, almost happily, it seemed, as if to reminisce about the loss of one's country was something they revelled in and looked forward to.

It will come as no surprise to any of you to hear that I am descended from an anti-confederate family, though I'll again defer to my father's terminology and say that my immediate ancestors were "pro-independents."

They were *for* something, my father said, something

that was *worth* being for. I was into my late thirties before I was able to at least partly answer the question of why my father and his brothers and sisters could not let go of what they called "the lost just cause of independence." And before that I at least partly understood how much more than mere politics or even patriotism was, for them, bound up in the matter of Confederation.

My father, or at least a character like him, has turned up in every one of my books, sometimes as a major character, sometimes as a minor one.

In my still controversial historical novel, *The Colony of Unrequited Dreams*, I put into the mouth of Joey Smallwood's father, Charlie, words that I heard from my father's mouth. The first chapter of that book is dominated by the blustering, self-pitying, eloquent, hard-drinking Charlie, of whom the narrator, Joey Smallwood, says: "He spent most of his meager wages on cheap West Indian rum which he bought from foreign sailors on the dock. When drunk he wandered about the house, cursing and mocking the name of Smallwood. He had been told by someone, or had read somewhere, that the name was from the Anglo-Saxon and meant something like 'treeless' or 'place where no trees grow.' It wouldn't have been a bad name for Newfoundland."

So there you have my father's words in the mouth of Joey Smallwood's father, which, my father has often pointed out to me, casts me in the role of Joey Smallwood, whom he believes that I, as he puts it, "let off too easily" in *The Colony of Unrequited Dreams*.

Of course, it was not my intention in that book to either *get* Smallwood or to let him off. My father's objection derives in part from my having written the book in first person and therefore, as my father says, letting Smallwood shoot his mouth off for almost six hundred pages.

In my father's estimation at least, I "made up for" *The Colony of Unrequited Dreams* in my memoir, *Baltimore's Mansion*. My father is unmistakably "in" that book, by name, and in an undisguised biographical sense, as is his father, my grandfather, Charlie Johnston.

There is a story about the writing of *Baltimore's Mansion* that I would find far-fetched to the point of being literally beyond belief had the events portrayed in it not happened to me.

I never tell anyone, not even my wife, or best friends, or editors, or publishers, or agents, anything about my works-in-progress. I superstitiously think that, if talked about before it is "done," a book will either come out wrong or evaporate altogether. I have never forgotten Robertson Davies' warning to would-be novelists that "more novels have been talked out in Irish bars than have ever been written in Ireland."

The day I finished *Baltimore's Mansion*, my father, who knew nothing of what I'd been writing for the past few months, phoned me from St. John's. He often recommends to me, for "filling out," his own plots that usually have to do with alien spaceships that have landed on Signal Hill or bent-on-mastering-the-world mutants born of secret American military experiments.

But on this day, he said something like the following: "Wayne, I have an idea for a book. Why don't you write a real story, one about Charlie and me and you?" The hair on the back of my neck stood up, as must the hair on the back of his when I replied: "Dad, you're not going to believe this, but I just finished writing that very book."

I mentioned the passage from *The Colony of Unrequited Dreams* for another reason that represents not only my father's attitude toward Newfoundland but that of — and I may be castigated for saying so — all Newfoundlanders.

Charlie Smallwood believes that he is doomed to failure by virtue of having been born a Newfoundlander. There were times when Joey Smallwood, mine and the actual historical figure, believed the same.

Once Smallwood was in power, he was often so ashamed of the backwardness of Newfoundland in comparison with other countries that he would apologize for that backwardness when visiting world leaders, premiers from other provinces, and businessmen who were all too quick to take his measure and his money.

There are *two* animating myths of Newfoundland. The first and most evident one derives from a sense of grievance and great pride. The best way I can think of putting it is that "The true king is always in exile while some pretender holds the throne."

In other words, Newfoundlanders believe themselves to be an intrinsically great people who, throughout their history, have been wrongfully prevented from enjoying the spoils of their greatness.

The other animating myth — and it is one that is rarely acknowledged in any quarter — is that Newfoundlanders are intrinsically inferior to other peoples of the world and have therefore been the authors of their own misfortunes.

In my memoir, *Baltimore's Mansion*, which tells much of the life of my father and grandfather and some of my own as it relates to buried nationhood, I quote my Aunt Freda, whose formal education was far more advanced than that of her siblings. She said: "Once we had a country, but because we made a mess of it, the British took it back."

She said that, from 1855–1934, Newfoundland was a self-governing colony of Britain.

"'Self-governing colony of Britain,'" my father said, "is just a fancy phrase for country." But Freda shook her head.

"No," she said, "we were never a country. And it was our own, it was we who ran the colony into the ground, bankrupted it through corruption and ineptitude. We forced the British to step in to bail us out before we were so far gone that we were beyond help."

"No," my father said, "it was because we spent so much helping Britain win World War I that we nearly went bankrupt. From 1934–1946, the British were in charge of us because they just took over."

"They took over because we were bankrupting *them*," Freda said. "They took over because we invited them to."

My father shook his head and asked her to remember the slaughter of Newfoundlanders at the Battle of Beaumont Hamel, considered by the British to have been "a minor squirmish" in the Battle of the Somme. Nine hundred of the Newfoundland Regiment's nine hundred and fifty men were wiped out, killed, or injured, in less than thirty minutes.

Freda shook her head. "Beaumont Hamel was terrible," she said, "but it doesn't change the facts."

But my father ignored her. Speaking of Confederation, he said, "Even with it rigged they barely won," as if the nearness of the vote — fifty-one percent to forty-nine percent — somehow proved that it was rigged, fixed, rumours of ballot boxes stuffed with the ballots of people who were dead or had never existed, confederates counting the votes, bribed election officials.

"I'll tell you this," my father said, "if our side had won and Peter Cashin had become prime minister — "

"He would have done away with fog and drizzle," someone said. Not Freda, but yet one more dissenting voice.

So there it was, not so simple after all. The cause, the lost just cause which possibly was lost because of some flaw or weakness in ourselves, because we had failed. Failure. All the bluster and bravado could not drown out that word.

It was because of the two animating myths of Newfoundland that I chose Joey Smallwood as the protagonist of *The Colony of Unrequited Dreams*. A megalomaniac with an inferiority complex. In a way the quintessential Newfoundlander. But not a Newfoundlander that I could ever be content in thinking as quintessential.

In all of Newfoundland history, which I scoured for months, auditioning for the role of my main character such great Newfoundlanders as Judge D.W. Prowse, the author of what to this day remains the authoritative history of Newfoundland, and Sir Robert Bond, Newfoundland's greatest prime minister and the first one born in

Newfoundland, I could not find the man who seemed as estimable as Smallwood, or one who embodied a third view of Newfoundlanders, the one I held myself but had so far not been able to personify.

So I made up a character. One I hoped would rival Smallwood and then some.

But not a man, a woman. Sheilagh Fielding who, in *The Colony of Unrequited Dreams*, is Smallwood's platonic lover, his greatest critic, best friend, and nemesis. Sheilagh Fielding who, in that book, gets the first and last word.

I alluded earlier to the still ongoing controversy regarding *The Colony of Unrequited Dreams*. I don't want to directly address the question of the rightness or wrongness of combining history, especially contemporary history, and fiction in a novel, mainly because its rightness or justifiability seems self-evident to me.

Once, at a reading, during the question period, I was asked by a history student, "How can you just mix people who really existed with people who didn't?"

I replied, "It's very simple. First you do it. And then it's done."

It's the best answer to that particular question I've ever come up with. And I have frequently answered it. In fact, I have more than once been told to answer it or else.

I was interviewed live by the CBC television station in St. John's. I was in Toronto, wearing headphones and staring into the blank, dark circle of a camera. No one else was in the entire studio.

The questions from St. John's began, the first being something like, "Did you know, Mr. Johnston, that the Smallwood family is quite upset about your book?"

Up to that point, I hadn't known and said so. I was then told by the interviewer what I had not been told before the interview, which was that he had just interviewed, live, as they sat on a sofa in one of their homes, several members of the Smallwood family, who had said many uncomplimentary things about me and my book.

I tried to keep my composure, never having been so blatantly blindsided by a journalist in my life and unable to rid my mind of the thought that the Smallwood interview and mine were on live TV.

I fumbled my way through the interview and went home in a daze where I found that there were twenty-seven messages on my answering machine, most of them from friends of mine in St. John's who had called to commiserate, and some from strangers in St. John's who, somehow having got hold of my unlisted number, had by no means called to commiserate.

There was a message from a woman who identified herself as a Smallwood and, weeping profusely, declared that Charlie Smallwood was a saint who had never taken a drink in his life. I felt lower than the lowest bit of vermin that had ever crawled the earth. As my sense of self-worth plummeted further, the voice changed to one that said, "Hi, Wayne. This is your friend, Claire. I hope you weren't taken in by my impersonation...."

When I toured the United States with *The*

Colony of Unrequited Dreams, I was much less apprehensive, especially in certain places where it seemed impossible that anyone who had even heard of Smallwood would be in the audience for a reading or book signing.

I read at Amherst College in Massachusetts, Amherst being famous for nothing but that it was the place where the poet, Emily Dickinson, was born and had spent her entire life.

As I read, now and then looking up to make eye contact with the audience, I peripherally saw several objects looming and swaying in mid-air. I kept on reading, not looking to my right or left but straight ahead. And those amorphous objects kept on looming and swaying.

Finally, I looked left to see, in the front row, three women holding, in political-convention-floor fashion, life-sized effigies of Joey Smallwood affixed to pieces of wood, complete with bow tie and horn-rimmed spectacles.

I stopped reading and asked for an explanation.

"We don't know anything about Newfoundland," one of the women said. "But, after we read your book, we went there. We went to Gambo where Mr. Smallwood was born. There's a kind of museum there and we bought some miniature Smallwood dolls. Our hobby is making life-sized likenesses of American presidents, which we place in chairs around our houses, but we decided, in honour of your book, to make some of Mr. Smallwood, too."

I left the reading picturing the houses of these

women, the rooms in which there were chairs
in which there silently sat likenesses of George
Washington, Abraham Lincoln, and Franklin
Roosevelt, among others, and, sitting among them,
as he would so dearly have liked to do in life, Joey
Smallwood, Premier of Newfoundland.

I was asked to give a reading in St. John's at a conference
whose ostensible purpose was to recognize the fiftieth
anniversary of Confederation. This was in 1999, and I
agreed to read on condition that I do so on April Fool's
Day, by which time *The Colony of Unrequited Dreams* would
have been out seven months.

I had made as few public appearances in St. John's
as possible, owing to the vitriolic controversy about the
book that had been raging since long before the book was
published and anyone but my editor had had a chance
to read it. It seemed that the very idea of fictionalizing
Smallwood's life had offended people, as if any alteration
of perfection could only mar perfection. There were also
advance rumours about a character with whom Smallwood had had an affair.

I was to read at a dinner for several hundred people at
seven in the evening. During the day of my reading, the
National Convention was reenacted. Smallwood had been
leader of the confederates at the National Convention
from 1946–1948, often filibustering for more than twenty
hours at a stretch and sucking on lemon wedges to ward
off laryngitis.

The National Convention was a temporary assembly
elected to determine what forms of government should

be offered to the people of Newfoundland in a referendum. The Convention voted not to include Confederation with Canada on the ballot, but Whitehall ruled that it should be included anyway. The other two choices were a continuation of Commission of Government or outright independence.

The anti-confederates knew what they were against, but could not agree what they were for—and this may have proved to be their undoing. For a while, there were various contending factions of anti-confederates, including one called "Economic Union" that favoured some sort of union between Newfoundland and the United States and was led by Chesley Crosbie. Economic Union's fortunes died quickly in the US Senate when some senator asked a colleague who had forwarded a motion to debate the possibility of making Newfoundland a state of the union: "Exactly why would we want to do that?

Another faction was led by Major Peter Cashin, a WWI hero, who underestimated the confederate threat and thought that some form of colonialism was his biggest foe.

Smallwood was allowed to "rave on" at the Convention, in part because Cashin did not have his oratory stamina, and in part because Smallwood was regarded as a mere crank whose cause— Confederation—could not possibly succeed.

There still exist, however, audiotapes of the Convention, and no one who has heard them has ever failed to be stirred by Cashin's fiery, heartfelt eloquence, nor to be bemused by his claim to have proof that a conspiracy against Newfoundland independence was afoot. (In 1947, my Aunt Marg was in such a hurry to get home to hear the Major speak that she fell and broke her leg.) Cashin never produced the proof and historians are still in search of it, at least one of whom believes he has found it and has written a book to that effect.

I thought it wise that I not attend the reenactment of the Convention, but I was later told in great detail of what went on there. Some who took part had actually been members of the Convention, while the rest were local actors.

Things began as planned. All the participants read verbatim from their scripts and the audience sat in silence. But as the debate went on, both the audience and the cast became more animated, the cast departing from their scripts to hurl epithets at their opponents, the audience urging them on.

Eventually the whole thing became just the sort of bitter shouting match that the National Convention had been day after day and night after night, the actor playing Smallwood so frustrating with his verbosity toward the actor playing Cashin that the latter had to be restrained from violence.

The reenactment of the National Convention ended at about four o'clock in the afternoon and was followed by a prolonged cocktail party, which was attended by both audience and cast who were collectively to make up my audience for the evening.

My reading took place at the Colony Club, which was

built by the Americans during the war and at one time had been a popular nightclub. It was now a special occasion banquet hall, and I was assured that it had not been chosen because its name and that of my book shared the word "Colony."

I never eat dinner before a reading and did not do so on this occasion. Nor did I sit idly at a table, as I often do at pre-reading dinners, but stayed backstage, listening to the excited hubbub out front, by the tone of which I knew what I was in for.

I perversely decided that if the crowd had come to voice their disapproval of me and my book, I might as well do my very best to incite them. After being introduced and coming onstage to a mixture of applause and catcalls, I read the parts of *The Colony of Unrequited Dreams* that I thought would offend as many people as possible: Smallwood asking Fielding to marry him in New York; Smallwood administering to himself, so to speak, during a long and lonely trek along the south coast of Newfoundland; Smallwood so bored with family life that he went out driving every night to avoid his wife and children.

I concluded my reading to the same mixture of applause and catcalls as had followed my introduction. The moderator wondered if there were any questions.

Seemingly en masse, the entire crowd stood up, hands raised, some people leaping up and down or shaking their fists.

Above the clamour, however, one voice rang out cold and clearly. It was that of a professor emeritus of English Literature at Memorial University who said, "Would you treat Jesus Christ in this fashion?"

After briefly pausing to reflect on the fact of a Newfoundland politician having achieved such stature in the mind of anyone, let alone someone encumbered with a PhD, I gave the kind of reply that usually occurs to me too late, in the car on the way home, perhaps, or while drifting off to sleep.

"Professor ..." I said, "it's apparent that you're a fan of both Jesus Christ and Joey Smallwood. In the latter's case, you should consider yourself lucky because they haven't based a Broadway musical on his life yet."

The uproar in the Colony Club was deafening until everyone suddenly fell quiet at the sight of the cane-encumbered professor who was making his way up the middle aisle between the dinner tables, his eyes unambiguously focused on me.

As he drew nearer to the dais, I tried in vain to imagine a way in which this could end well for me. I thrash a professor in front of five hundred people. A professor emeritus thrashes me in front of five hundred people.

What I didn't foresee was that a local politician, who was sympathetic to my cause, would intervene, a very large local politician who came up behind the professor, took him beneath the arms, and dragged him back the way he had come. The last I saw of the professor was the receding soles of his shoes.

There were no more advances upon the dais, but I did not succeed in winning over more than a few dozen of the people who were there.

After the reading, an elderly woman named Grace Sparkes, who had been an opponent of

Confederation, a journalist who relentlessly criticized in her newspaper columns every move made by Smallwood and his post-confederation government, and the person largely believed to be the model for my character, Sheilagh Fielding, approached me and said: "Mr. Johnston. I am told that I am widely believed to be the inspiration for Sheilagh. Don't worry, I'm not going to sue you or anything. I don't mind being mistaken for someone who gets off so many good one-liners at the expense of so many people who deserve them. What I do mind is the idea that people think I would ever have even considered sleeping with Joey Smallwood."

On another occasion, my Dutch translators, who had been sent to St. John's by my publisher to get the "feel" of the place, called me at my home in Toronto to say that they were in a bar called The Ship Inn in St. John's and that, even as they spoke, were looking at Sheilagh Fielding. I reminded them that Sheilagh Fielding did not exist. But they would not be put off.

"She's very tall," they said. "She walks with a limp. And a cane. And though she looks as if she's led a hard life, you can tell that she was once quite beautiful. And she smokes and drinks an awful lot, too."

After telling my translators that this last remark meant that they might be looking at almost any living Newfoundlander, I reminded them—it having just occurred to me—that this was Halloween and

that they were obviously looking at someone who
was wearing a Sheilagh Fielding costume.

So the controversy about my book continued. On a radio talk show, I was asked how it felt to know that I would be the cause of the mis-education and misinformation of future generations of Newfoundlanders, credulous children who would mistake my novel for a book of history.

I replied that it was easy to tell a novel from a book of history because the words "a novel" appeared on the cover of a novel.

I was asked if I could name any writers of note who had mixed history and fiction as I had. The caller seemed unimpressed with my reply, which consisted of a list that included Homer, Shakespeare, and Dickens.

I like to think that the tide finally turned in my favour when John Crosby was interviewed by the CBC radio network. Crosby was a one-time protégé of Smallwood who had crossed the floor from the Liberals to the Progressive Conservatives, thereby incurring the lifelong wrath of Smallwood. No one was considered to know Smallwood better than Crosby did.

The interviewer asked Crosby what he thought of my book. Crosby said he liked it. But what about this question of mixing history and fiction? the interviewer said, to which Crosby famously replied:

"Look. I don't know what all the fuss is about. The book paints a sympathetic portrait of Joey Smallwood, so it goes without saying that it must be fiction."

The subtitle of my lecture is "Family, Memory, Fiction, and Myth."

There is a comma between family and memory, but there may as well not be, for the two are, in my mind, indistinguishable. Much of what we think we remember from our pre-teen years is supplied by our parents and mixes with what we really do remember to form more elaborate "memories" in which truth and fiction can never be disentangled.

My own pre-teen years. I remember my uncle Harold reenacting, when I was four, the televised death of Lee Harvey Oswald. At least I think I do. My mother swears I was kept from watching TV for months after Kennedy was assassinated.

I am sure that I remember Kennedy's death being mourned by the nuns who taught us in school. I am sure that I can remember them crying because the man they called "our president" was dead. But there was no kindergarten in Newfoundland when I was four, so I hadn't yet started school by the time of Kennedy's death and so must have borrowed as my own a story told to me by one of my older brothers.

However those early memories came about, they caused me to think of myself as an American. If the American president was our president, I must be American.

I don't remember when I discovered that the nuns called Kennedy our president because he was Catholic. I do remember that this discovery was like finding out by accident that Santa Claus did not exist.

The nuns did not tell us we were Canadian. This is where Newfoundland's Confederation with Canada first manifests itself in *my* life. The anti-confederate side in the referendum was largely composed of Catholics from the Avalon Peninsula on the east coast of which St. John's is located. The nuns did not tell us we were Canadian because our having lost the referendum was one of those things that must not be mentioned.

Taboo.

In the lobby of our school hung pictures of Kennedy and whichever Pope was in power. Catholicism was our nationality. Canada was merely part of the nebulous elsewhere known as the outside world, which none of us had ever seen and didn't really believe in and certainly did not associate with what we saw on TV.

Lyndon B. Johnson was the American president. Lester B. Pearson was the Canadian prime minister. Lyndon B. and Lester B. They were interchangeable, irrelevant, two men about whom I knew nothing but that they had the same first two initials and their names ended with "son."

There was no Newfoundland history in our history courses. It was as if, for every child, Newfoundland history began with his or her earliest true memory.

But then my father's life intervened again.

By the time I was ten, he was all too aware of the contradiction that was his life. He had gone to agricultural college in Nova Scotia to earn a diploma in farming technology and returned to Newfoundland to find that the predicted flourishing of a new farming industry had not occurred and never would. And so the only technologist job he could get was with the Department of Fisheries, which was doubly ironic because his main reason for attending agricultural college had been to eschew all connection with the fishery, and second because the job he had no choice but to accept was with the *Federal*

Fisheries, also known as the *Canadian* Fisheries, which had begun operations in Newfoundland after the country's Confederation with Canada, which he and his family had so bitterly opposed.

"They're phasing out the train," he said, looking up from his newspaper one evening in the fall of 1968.

After Confederation, the Newfoundland Railway had been taken over by Canadian National Railways, CNR, which had just decided to replace the train with a supposedly more efficient, less expensive fleet of buses.

My father told me that unless you had seen Newfoundland by train you had never seen it, as the tracks took a much different route than the recently completed highway. The train was a reminder of his first train off the island in 1948. For him each train trip across the island was a recapitulation of that first one, which had been for him a strange hybrid of arrival and departure, discovery and abandonment.

And yet the subject of that first train trip was for some reason avoided in our family, my mother sometimes warning us children that we must never ask our father about it.

For a while it seemed that our whole family would join my father in a commemorative train trip across the island, my mother and we children experiencing for the first time the journey that, according to my father, invoked pre-confederate Newfoundland as nothing else could.

It also invoked, as many other things could, Newfoundland's history of backing white elephant industrial mega-projects and thereby being bilked out of millions, sometimes billions, of dollars by entrepreneurial "businessmen" from elsewhere.

The Newfoundland Railway was, for many years, called the Reid Railway, after the family from Montreal who were contracted to build it by the government of Newfoundland.

The Reid Contract, the first of many infamously one-sided contracts co-signed by Newfoundland, gave to the Reids, in perpetuity, "all rights" within thirty miles on either side of the railway track: water rights, mineral rights, development rights, etc. Added to this was a cash bonus for every mile of rail that was laid, and an overall cash bonus of tens of millions of dollars when the coast-to-coast project was completed. Post-confederate Newfoundland governments have been trying—unsuccessfully—for years to buy out the Reid family.

Newfoundland has, until recently, allowed itself to be directed by the Catch-22 dilemma of all underdeveloped nations. Lacking the money to develop its own natural resources, it has entered into agreements with other governments and large corporations who, in exchange for nearly all the royalties that derive from projects, fund those projects. All that Newfoundland has customarily received are short-term, low-paying, unskilled jobs.

Premier Smallwood negotiated with Hydro-Québec the Upper Churchill River Hydro Contract, which since about 1970 has seen Quebec make such profits by selling hydro-power to the state of New York—profits that would wipe out Newfoundland's entire fiscal debt of over ten billion dollars.

In the end, however, it was only my father and I who took the forty-eight hour return journey.

The trip was one long, train-borne party, the cars full of amateur musicians and mummers and passengers who drank openly from their own supplies of rum and beer. There was little for me to do but gape at the grownups.

The rival bus, which my father called the "blunder bus," was already running, and we sometimes saw it from the windows of the train, for sometimes the railway and the road almost converged. Children on the train stuck their tongues out at the bus, but what effect this had on anyone inside it we couldn't tell; its windows were tinted.

"It looks like a lunch bucket on wheels," my father said, and many people let out snorts of derision.

"It may not look like much," a man sitting several rows ahead of us said, "but it gets you where you want to go faster than this train does."

"Does it now?" my father said. "So what are you doing on the train if you love the bus so much?"

"Never said I loved the bus," the man said, "but we might just as well face facts."

"*Why* might we just as well face facts?" my father said. "If we all faced facts there'd be no one left in Newfoundland. There's nothing in the facts to keep us here. Is this what we've become, a country of fact-facing bus-boomers?"

"A province," the man said. "We're a province now, not a country. Never were a country, really, if you know your history."

"Is this what we'll have to listen to from here to Port aux Basques and back home again?" my father said.

"This fact-facing, blunder bus-booming, arse-kissing civil servant?"

My father all but spat out the last two words as if thereby expressing his distaste for his own occupation with the Federal Fisheries Department, trying in vain to rid himself of the self-contempt he had to live with every day.

The man said nothing, didn't even turn around, but it was all there in his silence: "We won. We won, and nothing you can say can change that fact, and nothing makes victory sweeter than the enduring bitterness of men like you."

My father fell into a brooding silence and, soon after, said that we should head to our berth for the rest of the afternoon. We sat side by side in the berth, looking out at the landscape, my father pouring himself glass after glass of rye and ginger ale.

"This is what I wanted you to see, Wayne," he said. "All of this."

He said he wanted me to see how much land there was, how like a country Newfoundland was in its dimensions and diversity.

In the days leading up to the trip, I had many times asked him, "How big is Newfoundland?" Using the map on the kitchen wall, he tried to make me understand how big it was, tried to give me some sense of how much more of it there was than I had seen so far in our drives around the bay.

"We're here," my father said, pointing at the tiny star that stood for St. John's. "Now, last Sunday, when we went out for our drive, we went this far." He moved his finger in a circle about an inch wide. Then he moved his hand slowly over the rest of the map. The paper crackled beneath his fingers. "Newfoundland is this much bigger than that," he said, making the motion with his hand again. "All this is Newfoundland, but it's not all like St. John's. Almost all of it is empty. No one lives there. No one's ever seen most of it."

The point of this journey was to get me away from the sea so that when I went back to living within two miles of it, I would know the land was there, the land whose capacity to inspire wonder in all who beheld it was in no way diminished by its being coloured the colour of Canada on maps.

When it was very late and the berth was dark and my father seemed to be asleep, I looked out the window at what, at that hour, I could see of Newfoundland, dark shapes of hills and trees, a glimpse, when the moon was out, of distant ice-caught ponds and lakes.

"We're passing through the core of it now," my father said, startling me.

I fell asleep and, some time later, was awakened by his voice, which was so low that I could not make out much of what he said.

But I did make out this much: "I wish I was there," he said. "I wish I never left. You should have kept your secret to yourself."

"Dad?" I said.

He froze in the act of raising his glass to his mouth. He lowered his arm.

"Thought you were asleep," he said.

"Who were you talking to?" I asked.

"No one," he said. "There's no one here but you and me."

"You were talking to your father, weren't you?" I said. "You were talking to Charlie." I knew little more about my grandfather than his name.

"Yes," my father said. "I was talking to Charlie. I often talk to Charlie. But he never answers back."

He didn't tell me Charlie's story that night. He told it to me in bits and pieces over the next ten years until I left what he still refers to as "the country."

Charlie Johnston was the lone blacksmith in Ferryland where my father was born, and where Charlie was born. Ferryland was, still is, the anti-confederate capital of Newfoundland. Major Peter Cashin, the leader of the anti-confederates, was born near there in a place called Cape Broyle.

After Smallwood was first elected premier and went on to win election after election by absurdly one-sided landslides, Ferryland held out and voted for the Progressive Conservatives as if in hope that the vote for Confederation could still somehow be overturned. It held out against Smallwood even after Smallwood said publicly, "I'm standing on the treasury box and Ferryland won't get one red cent until it votes for me."

Charlie Smallwood had been one of Cashin's lieutenants, helping the Major fight the doomed battle against Canada and Britain.

On referendum night, in July 1948, Charlie could not have been more devastated if his side had just been declared the losers in a winner-take-all war, if it had just surrendered to a regime to exist honourably under which would be impossible, and there was therefore nothing left for him to do but shoot himself.

When the last returns from Labrador came in, confirming the anti-confederate defeat, his wife, Nan, sat beside him and tried to console him at the kitchen table.

But he was inconsolable.

Just before midnight he went out and fired up the forge. He did not work or even burn anything, merely kept the fire roaring all night long, cranking the bellows to sustain that conflagration of protest, and drinking rum straight from the bottle.

He did this for nights on end.

Newfoundland was to be inducted into Confederation in March of 1949, but Charlie never lived to see it happen. One day, a longer than usual cessation of hammering on the anvil sent his wife out to the forge, where she found her husband lying on the floor, all his tools scattered around him. He was gone. Too soon for his own family to say goodbye.

But especially too soon for my father, who was away at college in Nova Scotia and did not have enough money to come home for his father's funeral. In my father's absence from Newfoundland, both his father and his country ceased to exist.

And this is the point at which family, memory, myth, and fiction all converge.

Everyone in my family knows that, as my mother often puts it, "something happened" between my father and Charlie the day my father left Ferryland for St. John's, where he caught the train for Port aux Basques and the mainland.

Something happened. Charlie's wife watched from her hilltop house as her husband and son met on the beach below. She saw them speak to one another and then saw Charlie turn away from his son and stride in anger up the hill toward the house.

What took place between them no one knows for certain. But the family myth is that one of them was a closet confederate.

When I was young, I had heard my father holding forth at parties about the closet confederates. There were many people, he said he was convinced, who had outwardly opposed Confederation, and indeed opposed it in their heart of hearts, but in the secrecy of the ballot box had voted for it. They had chosen pragmatism over patriotism.

"Imagine," my father said, "having to go your entire life living with a lie. Pretending to your wife or your father or your sister or your best friend that you were on their side, that you had voted with them but knowing, knowing in your heart of hearts, that in that voting booth, when no one else was looking, you betrayed them."

This was the myth. It was somehow comforting, reassuring to my father and the others, the impossible-to-verify idea that there existed this group of tortured, self-betraying souls.

Family, memory, and myth.

All that remains is fiction, yet fiction that is inextricably bound up with the other three.

There are two versions. In one, my father confesses to Charlie on the beach at Ferryland that he was a closet-confederate, that he faked his opposition to Confederation and in the ballot booth had voted for it.

In the other version, it is Charlie who confesses the

same thing to my father, confesses that he is one of the very traitors that he so bitterly condemned. Pragmatism over patriotism. One way or another, the family fiction goes, Confederation was the cause of Charlie's death.

I have several times asked my father if either version of the story is true, and his reply is always that the past is past, that back then things were different and there is no point now in trying to understand what happened long ago.

Family, memory, myth, and fiction still persist together, inextricably. And fiction is always, and sometimes blessedly, our story of last resort.

My parents, my aunts and uncles and their friends, are in their seventies and eighties now, and they are no less bewildered than they were back then.

After Confederation, they followed the river of what should have been, though they knew it led nowhere. Or that it led to nowhere but the Old Lost Land of Newfoundland.

AN EXCERPT FROM *THE COLONY OF UNREQUITED DREAMS*

We have joined a nation that we do not know, a nation that does not know us.

The river of what might have been still runs and there will never come a time when we do not hear it.

My life for forty years was a pair of rivers, the river that might have been beside the one that was.

On the day this country joined Confederation, I was hiding out from history, mine, yours, ours. I went back to a section shack on the Bonavista branch line that I once fled to years ago to write a book that I hope will one day be published. I stayed there for months, wondering, waiting — about what, for what, I hardly knew.

Wayne Johnston   45

I thought a lot about my parents: my American mother, who came from Newfoundland but went back home, without me or my father, when I was five; my father, who didn't know I knew that he betrayed me and thought that if I found out, I would no longer love him. He was wrong about that, as he was about so many things.

I sat alone in the section shack the night of the second referendum and listened as the results from each region were announced. The signal was weak, the numbers barely audible through a drone of static as if they were coming from a remote country I had heard of but never seen.

When I was certain the issue had been decided, I turned off the radio and went outdoors. There was a ladder on the side of the shack that led up to the roof, where I kept a rocking chair and where I liked to sit on nights when it was clear, as it was that night, to look at the stars and to watch the trains go by.

There was no wind. The moon, nearly full, was reflected in the ponds around the shack. I could see the glint of other ponds from what I guessed must have been ten miles away.

It was July, but it was cool enough that I could see my breath, and a sheen of condensation lay on everything. I sat in the chair, rocking slightly, imagining, as it was almost impossible not to do on such a night in such a place, that I was the sole person on the planet.

And that I heard the train, long before I usually did, long before it passed the shack, for the conductor, who was obviously a confederate, was blowing the whistle constantly. I saw the locomotive light far off in the distance.

For a while, it looked as though nothing but a light was coming, but then I saw the dark shape of the train.

It was not a passenger train. Perhaps it was a freight train with some cargo as oblivious to politics as the ponds that it was passing. Or perhaps this was a run purely for the sake of celebration, not so much of victory as the enemy's defeat.

For a few seconds there was nothing in the world but sound, the continuous blare of the whistle, the chugging of the train. The conductor saw me and waved his hat as he went by, grinning gleefully, as if he hoped I was an independent. To spite him, I waved back. I saw his mouth form the words We won.

What did he imagine we had won? What, had he "lost," would he have imagined he had lost?

I watched the train until it disappeared from view, the sound of the whistle receding. Something abiding, something prevailing, was restored.

I have often thought of that train hurling down the Bonavista like the victory express. And all around it the northern night, the barrens, the bogs, the rocks and ponds and hills of Newfoundland. The Straits of Belle Isle, from the island side of which I have seen the coast of Labrador.

These things, finally, primarily, are Newfoundland.

From a mind divesting itself of images, those of the land would be the last to go.

We are a people on whose minds these images have been imprinted.

We are a people in whose bodies old sea-seeking rivers roar with blood.

About the author

Wayne Johnston was born and raised in Goulds, Newfoundland. He obtained a BA in English from Memorial University and worked as a reporter for the *St. John's Daily News* before deciding to devote himself full-time to creative writing. Since then Johnston has written seven books and has been a contributing editor for *The Walrus*. His first book, *The Story of Bobby O'Malley*, won the WH Smith/Books in Canada First Novel Award. *Baltimore's Mansion*, a memoir dealing with his grandfather, his father, and himself, was tremendously well-received and won the prestigious Charles Taylor Prize for Literary Non-Fiction.

His novels *The Colony of Unrequited Dreams* and *The Navigator of New York* spent extended periods of time on bestseller lists in Canada and have been published in the US, Britain, Germany, Holland, China, and Spain. *Colony* was also identified by *The Globe and Mail* as one of the 100 most important Canadian books ever produced.

Johnston divides his time between Toronto and Roanoke, Virginia, where he has held the Distinguished Chair in Creative Writing at Hollins University since 2004.

About the Canadian Literature Centre

The Canadian Literature Centre | Centre de littérature canadienne was established at the University of Alberta in 2006. As the western hub of the Canadian literary community, it brings together researchers, authors, publishers, collectors, and the reading public. The Centre aims to promote literary research — in both English and French — representing diverse genres, languages, and regions of the country, and to foster public interest in Canadian literature with a view to enhancing an understanding of the richness and diversity of Canada's written culture.